A World Without End

For Robert Pinsky —
with thanks for your
visit to Indiana!

Best —

[illegible]

A World Without End

POEMS

Matthew Graham

THE RIVER CITY POETRY SERIES
VOLUME SIX

RIVER CITY
PUBLISHING
MONTGOMERY, ALABAMA

Published in the United States by River City Publishing.
1719 Mulberry St.
Montgomery, AL 36106.

Designed by Lissa Monroe.

First Edition—2005
Printed in the United States of America.
1 3 5 7 9 10 8 6 4 2

ISBN-13: 978-1-57966-050-5
ISBN-10-: 1-57966-050-9

Library of Congress Cataloging-in-Publication Data

Graham, Matthew, 1954-
A world without end : poems / Matthew Graham.— 1st ed.
p. cm. — (The River City poetry series)
Summary: "In the sixth volume of the River City Poetry Series, Matthew Graham muses over the stages of life and the entelechy of the human spirit, over the internal missions that are seeded within us from birth, and yet how our environments define and transform us"—Provided by publisher.
I. Title. II. Series.

PS3557.R216W67 2006
811'.54—dc22

2005029996

For Katie

In memory of Helen J. Graham

"… ye shall not be ashamed
nor confounded
world without end."
Isaiah 45:17

"Oh, dear departed days not so dear, just departed."
Henry Roth, *Requiem For Harlem*

Contents

III

IV

I

Two Grandfathers Fighting

He'd like to say
One grandfather took him often to see the great horses,
Clarence and Tom, mow endless pastures of timothy
Rippling in late summer heat.
Or that his other grandfather
Showed him off to his colleagues at the bank
When the El still rattled like profit over Water Street,
When men wore hats and women's legs whispered
In slanted light.
But he can't. One grandfather was a dark and silent man,
The other a nasty drunk.
Yet he carries them with him
With a certain affection. Some nights,
Dark and drunk, he smiles to think of his grandfathers
Arm wrestling within him. The farmer wins, of course,
But the banker has foreclosure capped
Inside his fountain pen.
All these struggles and foregone conclusions —
The sky boils over the countryside,
The cities are torn in half —
And his mind works in funny ways.
What's good about getting older?
You turn into men you thought you'd never know
While the world yammers on around you
Hilarious and hysterical.

Still Life With School Bus

On report card days,
During the atomic air raid drills of my childhood,
I pressed my face with the others
Hard against the sour concrete wall
Of the grade school's basement boys' room
And prayed it was real.

The afternoons slogged on,
Thick with fractions and flash cards,
And the wet wool of cloakrooms.
At three the old bus lurched out of the gloom
And I lined up with the others —
Clutching my plaid book bag
And that terrible card —
Perplexed by a world that promised to be,
But never was,
Swept clean.

First Dance

It was hot in the Catholic Junior High gym
And you felt miserable in your tight suit coat,
Downing warm Kool-Aid doled out in tiny paper cups
By the nuns lined up at the folding tables.
But somehow you found the courage
To ask her to dance when a Bobby Vinton number
Came up on the hi-fi.
For the first time in your life
You held a girl in your arms and confronted
Teased hair, and the wonder of straps and small stays.
You moved in close counterclockwise circles
Terrified of an erection, or of sweating through her dress,
Yet lost also,
Like a castaway coughed up on Paradise,
To the Shalimar and taffetta of girl.

Weeks later, when, in a moment that proved
Prophetic, two older guys held you
Over the hood of a GTO while a third
Beat the living crap out of you for dancing
With his girlfriend, you knew,
The joy of life's limits
Was in the testing.

When I Was a Kid

I thought pubic hair was public
And the perils of Tarzan were his pearls.
I'm still liable to dial 119.
In the late 1950s they didn't know from dyslexia.
You were just stupid
And got your head slammed against the blackboard.
I'm not complaining.
It made me humble and afraid to write.
It made me a quiet person on paper.
And forget about foreign words.
Once in Germany I ordered a pocketbook of coffee
And in a bar, told a Polish guy
I was a female professor.
Yet it all comes back to language,
That evil little dog at the door —
That brief flash we get
And translate as best we can.
Or as a French friend once said
To our boring host after an opulent dinner,
"Thank you. Thank you so much
For your hostility."

Childhood

We rode our beat-up bikes all over town.
My friend, Jimmy Freer, fat and serious,
Always behind, breathing a hard
"Hey, wait up."

My friend, Jimmy Freer, fat and serious.
Jimmy, concerned about the future —
"Hey, wait up" —
And what waited for him there.

Jimmy, concerned about the future.
I remember his little house
What waited for him there?
The yard strewn with car carcasses.

I remember his little house.
Inside it was crowded with babies.
The yard strewn with car carcasses.
Inside it smelled of urine and peanut butter.

Inside it was crowded with babies.
His mother, a big woman with a cigarette,
Smelled of urine and peanut butter.
His father, a shadow.

His mother, a big woman with a cigarette.
We skipped stones on the creek behind the bottling plant.
His father, a shadow.
We dreamed the crude summer away, riding all over town.

We'd skip stones on the creek behind the bottling plant.
Jimmy Freer, my friend who I laughed at behind his back,
Dreamed the crude summer away
And all of this is lost to me now.

Jimmy Freer, my friend who I laughed at behind his back,
Fell behind as people do in the years that came.
And while all of this is gone
That future rides heavy beside me now.

No Small Wonder

I'm collecting fireflies in a jelly jar
In our darkening back yard.
My father has punched holes in the lid
And padded the bottom with grass, though still,
The fireflies will all be dead by morning,
But I don't know that yet.
My parents are entertaining friends
And from the patio comes the trill and clatter
Of woman's laughter and ice in tall glasses.
It's way past my bedtime, but I seem to be forgotten
And that's fine for now.
Across the lake, the lights of the Hotel Jefferson
Pulsate like those on the ocean liner
I pretend I'll sail someday.
I'm eight years old and though nothing terrible has happened,
I sense I'll suffer for things I now know nothing about.
Suddenly, all my fireflies light at once,
And at the same time,
To the polite applause of the gathered friends,
My father flicks the switch to the Chinese lanterns
My mother has so sophisticatedly twined about the patio.
(Years later
They hang from the side of my garage and my friends applaud
My taste for 50s kitsch.)
All that light of promise and wonder.
All that light that descends back now
To the silent waves from where it came.

Death Car

Earl Kohler owned an Esso station
Next to my grandfather's house, outside of town.
Fat Earl chawed the stump of a wet cigar and worked
In the open maws of exhausted cars, while Willis,
His hired man, pumped gas and fixed tires.
Time passed in the shallow snores of a yellow dog
Named Zeke, asleep in the shade of the air pump.
Bees drifted in the hollyhocks along the garage
And the office was crammed with cracked cylinder heads,
Oil cans, and an empty candy counter, its glass front smeared
And fly-specked. A half-naked woman
Lounged on a 1949 auto parts calendar.

The night Earl towed in the death car,
He covered it with a tarp that the large lights
Of his wrecker splashed white and red.
The next afternoon most of our small town
Drove by to witness the tarped, crumpled,
Leaking thing that shut the stores and filled the church.
I watched from under my grandfather's porch,
Playing war with my plastic army men.
"Rubberneckers," my grandfather said,
To no one, from the porch above.
Most adult voices came to me then
From above. But later that day he looked
Under the tarp Earl quickly pulled back. And much later,

When the parade went home, and grandpa napped,
And Earl took his supper —

Sometimes I see the death car come alive.
A 1953 Olds 98 convertible coupe — headlights flaring,
The big V8 rocking the chassis — roars out
Of the Lake Jefferson parking lot spraying gravel.
(The state police have not yet called Earl,
Asleep in his small room above the garage.)
The long gold car opens up on the straightaway
Under lost stars. In the back seat sweats
A half-case of Black Label. In the front
A girl, between two boys, drapes her thin arms
Over their sunburned shoulders. Her neck —
A handblown stem of white glass — is arched back
To the wind and her own brief history.
She can smell the night, the lake, and the deep
Power of the car. The boys are eighteen, friends
And rivals for the girl who is seventeen and clever.
They make the first turn out of the straightaway,
But in the second, above the shale pits,
The death car is airborne. And in that stalled moment,
In that odd silence, its tail lights resemble
The afterburners of the rockets young lives
Are advertised to be.

Dark Star —
Death Car —
First star I see tonight.
Look after Earl, and Willis, and Zeke,
The kids in the Olds, my grandfather,
And the boy under the porch, watching.

Last Dance

Vinnie Ventura and the Thunderbirds always ended their last set
With a drawn-out version of *Time Is On My Side,*
So you could have one last slow dance
Before going home.
In the blue lights of the Delaware Valley Youth Hall
Vinnie Ventura, with his big red Gibson and his tenor voice,
Had the kids shuffling against each other
By the close of the night. In real life, Vinnie Ventura
Was twenty-year-old Vincent Marco Venterina, and like his dad,
Delivered mail. Heavyset, with an overcast face
And an out-of-style DA, he looked angelic
Those nights in that summer of staying or no coming back.

You always say, you wanna be free.
But you'll come a running back
You'll come a running back
You'll come a running back
To me.

That was the summer body counts climbed higher and closer.
The summer of small towns where Irish and Italian kids
Went after each other, sometimes with chains and stones
In empty parking lots, just for the hell of it.
And you learned to run, to talk fast,
To throw jokes before punches.

And you felt sure you'd never grow old
With the girl in your arms, or your deadbeat friends
Goosing each other by the fire doors.
Because you believed that beyond the youth hall, and the river,
And all that stalled farm land
Lay great cities with boulevards of threaded light,
Believed the night didn't end with the Thunderbirds' last set,
Believed Time, Time, Time,
Time was on your side —
Yes you did.

II

Meteorology

"I love this body/made to weather the storm/in the brain . . ."
—Yusef Komunyaka

The crescent in my eyebrow — a blind-sided
Slap shot before the vanity of head gear.

The question mark on my upper lip — a high school
Ring on the fist of a greaser with a grudge.

The lightning streaks on my left forearm — a windshield
At 50, splintered by desire.

The railroad tracks on my left knuckles — a road-crew
Chainsaw and a tree with a spike-nail surprise.

The raised cartwheel on the inside of my arm — a tattoo
From the deep fry of one-too-many kitchens.

The blue crease on my right ankle — an object lesson
In drunkenness and barbed wire on a lost Fourth of July.

The sly smile on my right wrist — a knife
In the night outside the Monteleone.

Lucky so far these fronts, these highs and lows,
Have been this forgiving to the landscape below.

Eager Street

I'll tell you this. After so many years
I still sometimes see myself
Walking up Eager in falling light,
Hugging my old brown overcoat.
I'm coming home from a late lunch shift
At the Owl Bar in the Belvedere Hotel.
The Owl Bar — a happy haunt
For Fitzgerald before the money went away,
Before Shepard Pratt and all that trouble there.
My happy haunt, while it lasted,
Mixing Old Fashioneds for retired ad men
And powdered dowagers in their dark banquettes,
The little table lamps turned low.
And old Eager Street — all marble
Stoops and terra cotta gargoyles guarding
Our brick apartment building.
I'll fix a drink and count my tips
At the kitchen table, the radio turned low
To *Little Larry's Afternoon Jazz Flight.*
And maybe later, if you're not there,
I'll head back downtown,
Sip an ouzo on the rocks in the Club Aeneas
And watch the naval officers at the coat check
Retrieve their golden swords.
Or I'll walk the harbor

And look at the Soviet grain ship
Moored there all week — its hammer-and-sickled
Smokestacks tattooed above the city
Like the cold war's worst nightmare.
The docks will be dark and deserted by then
And under pale street light I'll look
Like a character in a Goddard film, waiting for someone,
But I won't be.
Even then I was getting too old
To be that eager
To be left alone.

Famine

for Beiling

Outside, dogs barked and summer
Slipped by with the sound of baseball cards
Clothespinned to bicycle spokes
While all the T.V. dinners of the late 1950s
Grew cold on my plate
Until I was reminded with a slap
Of the starving children in China.
And I tried to imagine
A Chinese boy my age
Sitting in his Chinese house and dying
To be let out to play.
But all I had was my own mother,
Smoking and not speaking,
My father, an absence —
Time moving too slow and hunger,
All that hunger burning us.

Twenty years later I woke in Chinatown to a riot
Of sunlight and shadow caused by fire escapes
Clinging to the sides of yellow tenements.
Canal Street sang
With the commerce of smoke, shark fins and sea turtles.
To explain my departure, my absence of the night before,
I bought my woman friend a silk jacket, embroidered
With a purple dragon eating its own tail.

This did nothing to forestall the inevitable end
Of what was already ending as I walked away
From children playing off Mott Street,
Understanding nothing shouted to me,
That cold morning that foresaw so much.
I had not yet read Li T'ai Po.
I thought my thoughts were only my own.

It has not been that long really, since firepower
Flickered green in Tienanmen Square and on our television.
Tonight, I walk my dogs
While my wife reads, or doesn't, in our bedroom.
Few children sleep in the renovated homes I pass,
But of the ones that do, what starving children
Were they reminded of over tonight's uneaten food? What pictures
Will they take to the future? It's late fall, and though
We cannot burn leaves anymore, there is almost a taste
Of that past in the air. The past of possibility.
And me, I hunger
For nothing.

Easter Morning 1996

Hungover and alone
I place an old album on the turntable.
My revolutions are over
And nobody comes back from the dead
Except maybe in music.
From the window I see churchgoers
Circle for parking spots
Like pale birds of prey.
As a kid in church I was always distracted
By women in their Easter dresses.
For me, there the divine mysteries were concealed.

A late frost has shocked my azaleas
Into disbelief.
I notice this retrieving the Sunday paper
Full of its noise of advertising
And one-sentence paragraphs.
Brushing my teeth, I find even less meaning
In the bathroom mirror.
Spring forward, fall back. I change the clocks
And suddenly my rooms surrender to a song —
There's a somebody I'm longing to see,
I hope that she,
Turns out to be . . .

Rummage

October, 1995

The leaves scatter like golden coins
Over the last of the yard sales.
Fifty years ago guys named Joe
Rushed east in armor. Had time not stopped
For my uncle in a stunned and smoking tank,
He'd be seventy this year.
On one of the card tables I find
An embossed souvenir trivet
From the Century of Progress World's Fair.
Such hope in 1933.
I'll buy it for her.
We like things like this.

Birthday

My birthday and an unwanted surprise
Party in a restaurant from our past.
No snow in sight, just the blank bowl of the sky
Lowered over the traffic of assassins.
How much work she put into this plan. How cruel
I later become. And later, the lone walk outside
Through the yard and seized
Flower beds of the undeserving
And the cold comfort of weather.
Because of the clouds, the stars are gone.
Christmas, soon.
Blame the clouds.

March

I go running with the dog in the park
Under a heavy sky — a patina of shame.
Though the days are getting longer, they move still
Too fast and I wonder what we head toward,
What the point is,
Waiting up there. The park is empty
And my dog is disappointed, sniffing beneath the swing set
At half-frozen stuff.
She cannot begin to know how empty
A childless place can be, this time of year,
In late afternoon before spring
Has a chance to take its hold.

Anniversary

We leave the steaming salvage yard
Of marriage and travel north — enough milk
Under the bridge, tears over spilled water —
And find ourselves in a packet boat, in the iron-ore lanes,
Three miles off Copper Harbor.
There are more stars than we remember and I rename
The constellations: Cadillac de Ville, Hoover Upright, Man
Reluctantly Losing All He Loves. She sighs
And leans into the rail, stars in her hair and I spill
Styrofoamed coffee all over my hands.
Just hold me, she says,
And I do.

True Love

In late summer,
The last of the sun lights
The gable above my neighbor's porch.
It glows briefly then, almost an apparition,
As the yards and alley shut down in shadow.
This neighborhood, like any other —
Old houses with peeling garages
Tethered to small back yards by washlines,
The rose bushes and lilacs nurtured in the old way
With coffee grounds and egg shells.

And the frayed, faraway hem of traffic.

Some summer nights we bring light
Colored drinks to the back yard and wait
For a breeze from the river. Fireflies drift
In curtains.The dogs settle and sigh at our feet.
Inside there are books to be read
In the halo of light from above the bed.
There is tomorrow to think of. There are those we love,
And those we forget, finally, and those on the edge
Of our thoughts who come back at the oddest times.
Once, when all things slid and clicked in place,
It was time to leave.

True love
— Oh, lucky boy —
Is not leaving.

What It Comes Down To

It happened in the spring.
A false spring, true. Still,
Birth seemed almost possible
In that shifting season.

Then blood, and starlight
Slipped away from a very small star.

I even had, secretively, names
I liked. One was Tess.
The others don't matter.

Later
My wife cried on her hands and knees
On the kitchen floor.

Suddenly the whole world came down
To a woman crying.

The Sadness of Summer

Another summer gone.
The clapboard cottage swept clean.
Dust rises and falls along the back roads
Of September. Remember
The bouquets of Queen Ann's lace gracing the breakfast table
Beneath the sheer curtains of June?
There are no boats on the water today.
And as I looked at you in the yard
From the upstairs window, as I saw you bend
And clip the last of the wild daisies
And saw my own reflection,
I thought of all the years quietly gone
That we have touched together
And of the life that we have made
And worn
And have become together.

III

Shaker Door, Circa 1820

The burl of the sycamore still swirls
In this door, as this door once turned
Shut on a grinning, handshaking world
With its overland wagons of sin.
This door, open to celibacy,
To confession and separation
From the world we're still wandering in.

You gasp as I move in you, toward you,
Move you toward a closed door opening
On moonlight and the holy murmur
Of sycamores. Early fall. First frost.

Those long-gone Shakers sought redemption
In movement, and in their denial —
Simplicity. Still time turns us all
With commerce, with silence, and with prayer,
Toward the inevitable struggle
Between opening and closing,
Between the waiting and the going somewhere.

Valentine, Be Mine

London, February 15th, 2003

Walking with the crowd in the Strand
My wife tells me to keep my mouth shut,
Afraid our flat American voices may trigger
An unwanted response. But at this stage
The peace march is a holiday — kids dancing,
Families pushing prams, old couples in matching macs.
But there's seriousness here too
And I keep my eye on open alleys.
We are old enough to know
How these things can turn,
When the tear gas pops,
When the police move in.
The news helicopters that punctuate the lowered sky
Are memory enough.

Later, a little guiltily, we slip down to Gordon's
For a quiet wine with other marchers,
And with those who don't seem to know
What's been going on.
On the stone floor we find a heart-shaped card:
"To Babe, the sexiest chick in the world."
What's sadder than a discarded Valentine?

History?
(they marched here in 1914)
Or all the broken hearts
To be.

Angel Mounds

After visiting her mother,
After walking the old blocks of her childhood —
The ruined cinema where she first touched a boy,
The silent record store — and with the whole neighborhood
Falling beneath her, she's amazed
It ever meant anything.
Her mother is strong. But two years is not enough time
To leave behind her husband's death.
"Sometimes," her mother says, "when the wind
Blows real hard, I think I see your father
Standing out there by the garden."
She kisses her mother goodbye
And feels something shift in her own life
That she can't explain.
So she drives her husband's car,
Past the strip mall and the subdivisions
To a place that's never been explained.

It's a mound builder village — abandoned
Centuries ago, now run and protected
By the state and named not for spiritual beings,
But for the family that once owned the land.
She feels an affinity with a lost people
Who raised hills by hand
From a flood plain.
It's this land, she thinks as she walks

The fields toward the largest mound. *It's the loneliness*
Of land left behind that I love,
That returns me.
It's late November. The milkweed pods
Are broken and blown, and the trees
Carry with them the message of winter.

The wind blows and she imagines she sees them —
Gathered on the crest —
The women of the village, the last to leave.
As she watches they begin to rise,
Angels of shifting light and wind.
Angels of goodbye.
She opens her hand as they ascend
Slowly and finally,
With purpose and in a manner
All other women
Have learned to follow.

Looking for Levine in Detroit with Some Last Words from Henry Ford

He isn't in Greektown
Glaring at his coffee in a luncheonette off Monroe.
Or at the aquarium on Belle Isle where even the fish look desperate.
There's no hardboiled white character crossing
One of those blasted streets by Wayne State
Or further down on Mack Ave.,
Where you can get yourself seriously killed.
No, it's over on Kelly
In the Detroit Institute of Arts
Where you'll find him now.
Look at Diego Rivera's great fresco.
In the north panel, in the foreground
Of the Ford Motor Company Rouge Plant,
The face of the second man on the left
Pulling a dolly of engine blocks
Is the face of the future Levine.
Set in lime, sand and Marxist
Controversy, it's a face made noble
By what was once called honest work.
It's a face that can see beyond the Billet Mill
And the Bar Mill to the sunlit showrooms
Of the promised world.
All this of course was long before

The real Levine left town on a bus.
Before the labor punched him deaf and blind
And made him speak a language
Propelled by power generated
From within itself.

Two Small American Verses

Work

Ship yards, stock yards, transfer yards,
Lumber yards, coal yards, brick yards,
Salvage yards, junk yards, freight yards,
And the gas works, iron works, water works,
Steel works, oil works, vinegar works —

Remember always
Thy metal lunch pail, its thermos of coffee,
And blessed shalt thou be when thou comest in,
And blessed shalt thou be when thou goest out.

Street

Bail bonds, title loans, checks cashed, prepay before you pump,
No bills over 20, Adult Video, Fast Cash, Discount Liquor, O.T.B.
Scratch-N-Dent, Quick Mart, Trailways.

Down this lane you've relived
Your sorry way more than once.
Yet to repeat is to forgive
Forever in your thankful brain,
This stretch of street etched in rain.

The Wild Roses of the Outer Cape

Splash the side of the Truro Post Office
Where grumpy Edward Hopper bought his stamps.
Mister Hopper, to the locals, even now.
The roses are as prevalent as sand,
Ghost crabs, the shifting sky.
And that's the sadness of beauty —
Too much, and all you notice is its absence.

It's the Monday after the Fourth
And Truro's tiny post office is packed.
An old lady in line says,
"The Cape constantly rolls over itself."
Like memory, you think. Like Mr. Hopper in 1934
Staring all summer at one empty canvas.
A framed nothing. A landscape ravaged
By roses.

Lyles Station, Indiana

We take some pictures and look around.
A few trailers, a church, an abandoned school —
All that's left of this freed-slave community.
For a moment
Time becomes a wheel turning above us.
Its shadow brushes the lilacs
Outside the school's open door
And it enters with us,
Touches the blackboard listing the names
Of the men serving in Korea, and settles
On the rows of stacked wooden desks.
Our photos won't show the ceiling fan's dusty flutter,
The children seriously reading their donated
Healthy Home and Community books,
Or their young teacher, the light striking
His gold spectacles
As he looks up just now,
Toward some distraction in the doorway.

French Lick, Indiana

How many hand-stenciled railroad carriages
Stopped before this cracked concrete platform.
How many small, silk-stockinged feet
Stepped down in summer light.
How many tennis rackets.
How many hat boxes.
The ruined arch of the hotel entrance
Rises in the streaked sky
And casts its shade
Toward the future across the tracks.

Oh tanning salon, oh video store,
Oh brave used-car lot.

Petersburg, Indiana

Relax. It's only the wind

That moves the window pane,
That waters your eyes,
That makes dust devils dance in the road.
It's only the wind
That takes your hat,
The elementary school,
Half the houses,
And all the trees on Sycamore.

Relax. We have no secrets anymore.
They've all been blown across the fields
Like flocks of dead birds.
The cow jumped over the moon.
The plate ran away with the spoon.

Relax. That's only the CSX train.

And it's only the wind
That rattles the door,
Flickers the light,
And comes up the stairs
And causes the dogs
To sit up and howl.

And causes the dogs to howl.

Gettysburg

I first saw the village that hot morning
Through the scratched lens of Caleb's stolen field glass

And felt like a landlocked pirate peering from a ridge
At smoke rising from the summer kitchens,

A dray horse plodding up a brick street, birds circling
A church. I smelled biscuits and bacon and the hushed breath

Of another scorching day a-coming. Later,
I saw a cavalry charge swallowed by a field of smoke —

All that blue and gold and gold lace gone, and then
Sergeant Billy up close and screaming — "Bayonets

Ready. Heads down, lads. Don't bunch up and
Goddamn ye! Goddamn ye all to hell!"

Death touched me then on the cheek, but moved on
Because I was Jack Straw up from the slums of Albany

Two-fisted I was, and like me Da
The taste of steel in my mouth. The taste of the city.

And this was July in the country.
This was July outside a civil town

In my only country.
The only country I finally got to know.

Hué

for Jim McGarrah, Joe Sayyah, Keith Weisheit

"To live is to borrow. To die: a giving back."
—Ho Xuan Huong

After all these years
Little bits of them are still dredged up
From roped-off crash sites and river banks —
A chunk of bone, a buckle, a boot heel —
And sent home once more in body bags.
Yet all the king's horses
And all the king's men
Can't ever put them back together again.
What good are spent rounds, empty ammunition crates?

They were too young.
Too young to know
That the blue smoke that rose from the city of Hué,
Would change the complexion of the sky at dawn,
And sound forever the cry and alarm.

Cold War

for Sibylle Badstuebner

I. Liberty, New York 1963

The Weiss boys annexed new territory
In the neighborhood that winter
We couldn't eat snow because of the testing.
Then missiles locked on Miami and a Mercury space capsule
Sank at sea. That summer I lived with my grandmother,
I watched a lattice of sunlight
Slide along the porch.
When I returned the Weiss boys had moved.
An empty peace settled on the neighborhood,
And then somebody shot the president.

II. Karl Marx Platz, Berlin 1991

After stalling for time we departed
At a station whose time had come.
Its tile cornices were swirled
With the ash of a park burned for fuel.
Time watched from tired windows —
Rearranged by shrapnel and rain —
The distant boulevards widen with light.
Time bought time

Beneath blind surveillance cameras,
And in time whole districts surrendered.
Later, back on the street, with my watch
Stolen or lost, I begged pardon
For the time.

Venezia

It unfolds like the dark wings of a crusader's dream,
Like a torn banner in a sickly breeze.
It's a palace barely floating on rags of light
And the stolen bones of lost saints.
It's a plague ship marooned in a bright lagoon
Of terrorists and tourists, priests
And pickpockets. It's Tintoretto's
Marriage at Cana in the sacristy
Of the Basilica della Salute.
Women pour great urns of wine
While Christ is pushed to the back of an endless table
Crowded with freeloaders.
In front of an A.T.M.
It's a dropped bottle of good Brunello
That pools like blood
On the cobbled street watched over
By a boy soldier in body armor
Cradling a machine gun like a frightened child.
It's children playing soccer beneath washlines
In the bleached courtyards of late afternoon.
It's eavesdropping over Bellinis in Harry's Bar
Where two thieves converse.
"I conned my way into paradise,"
Says the good thief.
"The light grows golden,"
The bad thief replies.
"And God is everywhere."

St. Thomas, After Many Years, Speaks of Christ

Let me assure you, he was different when he returned,
A bit stern, yes, a bit adrift
And distracted. It was as if
He wasn't sure where he was.
And I understood that, but it was the doubt
That I first saw. A hole in the eyes
That showed a hint
Of that nightmare hill, long shadows,
And the black birds circling.
It was as if . . . well, I don't know.
But you get to know a man when you've poured
His wine, held his hand, helped him sit
Upon an aged burro with fly-crusted eyes
Standing on a stretch of blasted sand.
I knew this man. Then he went away again
And that was that. Those stories
About my hand and his side
Were made up later for the effect, but I
By then, had no doubt about the doubts
He might have had.

An Irish Ghazal

Near the unmarked post office recipes for revolution
Were studied in amber pub light.

Smoked salmon with watercress. The millstream and moss.
The ruined monastery in the mist. And the falling light.

On the Blasket Islands we eat soda bread with sharp cheddar cheese.
In the sand a sheep's skull is bleached communion-wafer white.

My grandfather, dead these thirty years, wheels his bicycle
Down a shaded lane speckled in sea light.

"Trees that go black against the sky
And then — how soon the night!"

There is a loneliness only love knows. You stand on the deck in the wind,
Watching the coast slip into the night.

Beneath a painting of St. Matthew, a table of cold cabbage
And gray ham is blessed with candlelight.

IV

Shelter Island

for Vic and Leah Friedman

In light late-summer rain
The old resorts remain.

Down still hallways wait
Rooms of rough towels and chifforobes
That smell faintly of the sea
And paper-wrapped bars of Cashmere Bouquet.
(The chipped enamel basins drip.)
On the veranda the lamps are lit
As sprays of sea birds stitch and soar
Above the concrete rasp of shuffleboard.

Out on the damp sand
Empty deck chairs are arranged
Like cocktail parties about to begin.
And as the light begins to fold
The sound of the waves
That command the Sound,
That move the ships across the Sound,
Collapse like clocks unwound.

Could we stay here awhile
Among this august disrepair?
Could we stay here sheltered awhile
From all the coming years' despair?

Dark Bay

In the albums all that changes are the faces.
See how they squint into a sun
Flaring again
Off Crow Island and into our eyes,
As the breeze that moved their shore
Rocks the rockers on the porch still.

In Dark Bay the boathouse still
Stands. Victorian and aloof it faces
The Adirondacks where a final shore
Separates our years from theirs as the sun
Divides the day. Our eyes
Adjust. There, the canvas canoe and again

Richard's runabout. Again
In need of repair. It still,
As in the photos, waits for Richard. His eyes
Smiling into time, and into the faces
Of friends come and gone with the sun
Of such a distant shore.

In the camera we face the shore and sun. Our eyes and hair again
Stilled and somewhat young.

News

Richard V. Hyatt 1923 – 1995

After my friend died it seemed unfair
The liquor store where he bought scotch
Remained untouched behind its blue surveillance.
Morning traffic argued on,
And the newspaper arrived on time.
I kept his music and watered his plants
As if he were on vacation
And when he'd return I'd say —
Nothing new since you've been gone.

But now the liquor store's torn down,
The new expressway slides past a harvest
Of fast food, and the paper girl went to college.
So much I need to report —
Charlie sold the car, Ole moved,
It rained all summer —
Since last you latched
The backyard gate.

Obituary

Say the names. Breathe them in.

Harriett Herbert Henry Gladys

Say them again, these names that came
With the beginning of the century

Frank Agnes Bernice Victor

And are leaving us now at the end.
How like ancient perennials they bloom
Once more in the back pages of the paper.

Dottie Henrietta Hazel Herman

Or how sometimes in spring, in a field,
A border of jonquils will rise up
In the shape of a house no longer there.

Beatrice Selma Trudy Isabelle

Remember what they meant. Breathe them out.

Offices

I read Robert Hayden's *Those Winter Sundays*
To my class and start to choke up,
But no one notices. I can't blame them.
They're young
And bored and know all they think
They need to know.
One kid suggests that maybe Robert
Didn't like his father very much
And that seems to end the discussion.
Though they are sure of anger and lonely,
They are not so sure of chronic or austere.
And what about those offices?
The class drifts away
But I think I can finally see that place.
The halls are dark.
The radiators gurgle and pop
Among the full file cabinets,
The Bakelite ashtrays and black rotary phones.
And on every cluttered desk
A Corona Silent waits.

Terminal

for Robert Wrigley

My father stands on the back stoop,
Smokes half a cigarette, butts it out
And pockets what's left. He's done this
For as long as I can remember,
Out of economy or some weird sense of health.
He coughs, spits and puts down a plate
Of scraps for the runaway neighborhood cats —
Homeless cats, he calls them.
I finish the dishes and watch
From the kitchen window. My mother has cancer
And lies on the couch in the den
Doing crossword puzzles. My father
Tries to put on a good front for my visit
But the whole house stiffens with her news.
"I'm so old I don't even buy green bananas,"
He used to say, but not anymore.
My old man, who never asked for anything,
Shoulders something new now that's too heavy
To move, too fragile to set down.
And what can I do but be here for awhile —
Help stack firewood, put away
The deck furniture —
As I wasn't after ancient battles
Over the length of my hair, the character
Of my friends and that war

Spreading toward us like a disease.
(I still think of young Sparky
Dropped in his tracks along the Perfume River.)
And I'm not sure how we survived
Those stupid days. Unbelievably
My mother calls from the den
For an eight-letter word meaning
Point of departure or arrival.
I drain the sink, flick off the kitchen light
And for a moment all I see from the window
Are a few stars tucked into the long night.
And then my father comes inside slapping his arms.
"It's going to be a cold one," he says.

History: A Prayer

And so they come to the scattering of her ashes
In a still lake by their old house.
In the distance a boy
Skips rocks along the dam. Clouds scribble their salutations
And closings across the sky. Oar locks creak
As oars dip, rise, and dip in late autumn light
And then rest as clumps of gray ash
Bloom white in the water and dissolve in the silence
They carry like a gift.
This too will soon become the distant past.
The boy by the dam is gone, called home to supper
By his mother, or just lost
In the haze below the trees.
Lost to a world without end —
It will be thirty-five years before he returns.

Let the past pour over the past
For all the days of our lives.

NOTES

Last Dance. The lyrics quoted are from "Time Is On My Side," written by Norman Meade.

Looking for Levine in Detroit with Some Last Words from Henry Ford. The quote is part of Henry Ford's description of the internal combustion engine.

Irish Ghazal. The quoted couplet is from Charlotte Mew's poem "On the Road to the Sea."

The Wild Roses of the Outer Cape. Some details are from Gail Levin's biography, *Edward Hopper.*

Easter Morning 1996. The lyrics quoted are from "Someone To Watch Over Me," written by George Gershwin.

ACKNOWLEDGMENTS

Cincinnati Poetry Review
Crab Orchard Review
Indiana Review
Harvard Magazine
River Styx
The Southern Indiana Review
Poet Lore

And What Rough Beast, Poems at the End of the Century
Edited by Robert McGovern and Stephen Haven

And Know This Place: Poetry of Indiana
Edited by Jenny Kander

Matthew Graham is the author of two books of poems, *New World Architecture* (Galileo Press, 1985) and *1946* (Galileo Press, 1991), and the recipient of awards and fellowships from the Academy of American Poets, the Indiana Arts Commission, Pushcart, and the Vermont Studio Center. He directs the creative writing program at the University of Southern Indiana where he codirects the RopeWalk Writers Retreat and is poetry editor of the *Southern Indiana Review.* He is married to the painter Katie Waters.